Bartholomew Roberts

by Sue Hamilton

Visit us at
www.abdopublishing.com

Published by ABDO Publishing Company, 4940 Viking Drive, Suite 622, Edina, Minnesota 55435.
Copyright ©2007 by Abdo Consulting Group, Inc. International copyrights reserved in all countries.
No part of this book may be reproduced in any form without written permission from the publisher.
ABDO & Daughters™ is a trademark and logo of ABDO Publishing Company.

Printed in the United States.

Editors: John Hamilton/Tad Bornhoft
Graphic Design: John Hamilton/Sue Hamilton
Cover Design: Neil Klinepier
Cover Illustration: Captain Bartholomew Roberts, Mariners' Museum; *Pegleg,* ©1996 Don Maitz
Interior Photos and Illustrations: p 3 *Dead Men Tell No Tales,* ©2003 Don Maitz; pp 4-5 Captain
Bartholomew Roberts, Mariners' Museum; p 6 *Insurrection On Board A Slave Ship,* courtesy British
Library; p 9 Bartholomew Roberts, Mariners' Museum; pp 10-11 Harbor in Africa, Mary Evans;
p 13 Gallant Bartholomew Roberts, Mariners' Museum; p 15 Fleet of ships, Corbis; p 17 Paper
scroll art, Zedcor; *Ahoy Maitz,* ©2002 Don Maitz; p 19 Flag, Zedcor; p 21 Hanging from the
yardarm, North Wind; p 23 Treasure chest, Mariners' Museum; p 24 Map of Roberts' range,
Cartesia/Hamilton; p 25 Buccaneer ship, Mariners' Museum; p 27 Royal Navy and pirate ships
battle, Mary Evans; p 28 Death of Roberts, Mariners' Museum; p 29 Skull and crossbones, Zedcor;
p 32 *Up the Anchor,* ©2002 Don Maitz

Library of Congress Cataloging-in-Publication Data

Hamilton, Sue L., 1959-
  Bartholomew Roberts / Sue Hamilton.
     p. cm. -- (Pirates)
  Includes index.
  ISBN-13: 978-1-59928-757-7
  ISBN-10: 1-59928-757-9
  1. Roberts, Bartholomew, 1682?-1722--Juvenile literature. 2. Pirates--Biography--Juvenile literature.
I. Title.

G537.R74H36 2007
910.4'5--dc22
  [B]

                           2006032011

Contents

Bartholomew Roberts

Bartholomew Roberts, also known as Black Bart, was the most successful pirate to sail the Atlantic Ocean. Bold and lethal, he terrorized both merchant and military ships, something other pirate captains would never do. He was fearless, ruthless, and smart, capturing an amazing 400 ships in less than four years.

Roberts did not fit the classic "pirate" label. He didn't drink, nor did he gamble. He dressed in fine fashion, often sporting a feathered hat. Rules for his crew were outlined in his pirates' code of conduct. He wore a diamond-studded cross, and encouraged his men to pray.

How did someone like this become a pirate? Chance brought him to the life of a sea raider; intelligence made him the most successful thief of the Golden Age of Piracy.

Above: Captain Bartholomew Roberts with two of his ships.

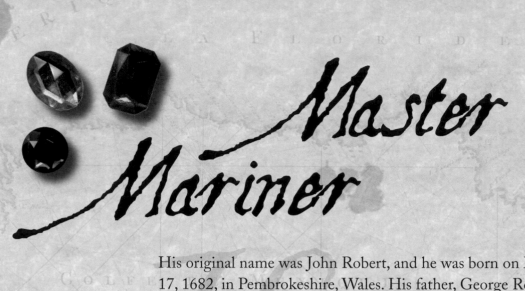

Master Mariner

His original name was John Robert, and he was born on May 17, 1682, in Pembrokeshire, Wales. His father, George Robert, was a landowner. John grew up as a working gentleman. However, farming the land was difficult, and not at all what John wanted to do. He was drawn to the sea. At a young age, he left the care of the land to his younger brother, William, and set off for adventure.

Young John Robert probably began his career as a deckhand, learning and growing on board various ships. He likely served in the British Royal Navy from 1702 to 1713, during the War of the Spanish Succession. He grew into a master mariner, a fine navigator and a strong leader.

Tall and dark, he is said to have been "of good natural parts and personal bravery." In other words, he was a handsome man who bravely took control.

After serving in the Royal Navy, he became a merchant seaman. Although honest and hard-working, he was a commoner, and likely would never make captain.

Robert was 37 years old and employed as the second mate aboard a ship called the *Princess of London,* a slave ship commanded by Captain Abraham Plumb. The ship set sail in November 1718, headed for the west coast of Africa to pick up a cargo of slaves.

Below: A slave ship from the 1700s.

Left: Captain Howell Davis. He invited John Robert to sail with him aboard the *Royal Rover.*

The unfortunate *Princess* arrived on the Guinea Coast at the same time as the 32-gun *Royal Rover,* commanded by Welsh pirate Captain Howell Davis. Davis plundered the *Princess.* The pirate captain also pressed some of the *Princess'* crew to join his raiders. As a master mariner, as well as a fellow Welshman, John Robert was invited to sail with the pirates. Robert reluctantly agreed.

John Robert likely had no choice but to turn pirate, although Captain Davis prided himself on not forcing anyone to join his ranks. Perhaps Robert was tired of hard work and little reward. He is quoted as saying, "In an honest Service, there is thin Commons, low Wages, and hard Labour; in this (pirating), Plenty and Satiety, Pleasure and Ease, Liberty and Power…."

However, in the pirate world, money and freedom are exchanged for danger and death. In a very short time, John Robert would witness this for himself.

Above: In 1719, John Robert turned pirate, joining the crew of fellow Welshman Howell Davis.

Black Barty

Accepting his role as pirate in 1719, John Robert changed his name to Bartholomew Roberts. Bartholomew may have been his middle name. He may have done it to protect his family. It may be that he wanted something more memorable than "John." Whatever the case, the tall, dark pirate would forever be known as Bartholomew "Black Bart" Roberts. Many of his shipmates called him Black Barty.

Roberts was quick to see that Howell Davis knew how to be a successful pirate. One of his least dangerous and most successful stunts occurred when Davis sailed his ship to a slaving company's fort by the mouth of the Gambia River on the west coast of Africa. The wily captain, along with two men, visited slave traders at the Royal African Company. Dressed in finery, they gained a dinner invitation from the governor. Unfortunately for the governor, the pirates promptly took him hostage, holding the embarrassed official for ransom. They sailed away with £2,000, a nice sum of money.

This clever stunt became widely known, making Davis a most-wanted man. It did not send the pirate captain into hiding, however. Instead, he partnered with two other pirates, Olivier la Bouche and Thomas Cocklyn, and continued raiding ships and forts. Roberts came to see the plundered wealth the pirates gained, including ivory, gold dust, and slaves. Unfortunately, they also made many powerful enemies.

Above: In 1719, John Robert turned pirate, changing his name to Bartholomew Roberts.

Below: Captain Howell Davis.

In June 1719, only about six weeks after Roberts joined Davis' crew, they sailed the *Royal Rover* to the Isle of Princes, also known as Príncipe, which was a Portuguese-controlled island off the west coast of Africa. After entering the island's harbor, Davis convinced Príncipe's Portuguese governor that he was a privateer, sent by the Royal Navy to rid the area of pirates. Davis even went so far as to take a French vessel that entered the harbor, claiming that he'd seen the captain and crew trading with pirates.

After successfully re-supplying his ship, Captain Davis received an invitation to the governor's palace. Although exact details are unknown, Davis was about to have the tables turned on him.

Left: A port on the coast of West Africa in the early 1700s.

Some say that Príncipe's governor had heard about the ransoming of the governor in the Royal African Company's fort. Others say the governor was warned by an islander who had learned about Davis' scheme. Whatever the case, the unsuspecting pirate walked into an ambush at the governor's palace. As Davis approached, hidden Portugese soldiers started shooting. Davis' body was blasted with five bullets. Just to be sure he was dead, the soldiers slit the pirate's throat.

The news soon reached the crew on board the *Royal Rover.* With no time to lose, they quickly sailed out of the harbor, fearful that Príncipe's cannons would be turned against them.

Once safely away, the crew had two tasks to attend to: elect a new leader, and take revenge for the death of their old captain.

Pirate Commander

In the late summer of 1719, the crew of the *Royal Rover* gathered to elect their new leader. One man had proven himself to be intelligent, fair, a master navigator, as well as skilled in warfare. Although he had only been among the pirates for a short time, Bartholomew Roberts was elected their captain.

Some, including the ship's quartermaster, Walter Kennedy, were angry about the decision. Kennedy likely expected to find himself voted in as captain. But he would abide by the crew's decision—at least for awhile.

Black Bart, when offered the captaincy, accepted the post, stating, "Since I hath dipped my hands in muddy water and must be a pirate, it is better being a commander than a common man."

Roberts quickly devised a plan to avenge Captain Davis' death. Only a week had passed when the *Royal Rover* sailed back to the island of Príncipe. Once there, brutal attacks were made on land, as well as from the sea. The town was shelled, burned, and raided. In short order, Roberts had proven himself a clever captain, as well as a powerful, merciless enemy.

Leaving the smoking ruins behind, Roberts sailed away from Príncipe. His next destination was across the Atlantic Ocean. Black Bart was headed for Brazil, South America. He had other continents to raid, and he was about to become one of the most successful pirates to sail the seas.

Above: Captain Roberts stands on deck armed with a sword and three pistols.

Portuguese Plunder

Before leaving Africa in 1719, Roberts and his men raided several ships filled with rich booty. But while sailing across the Atlantic Ocean toward South America, the pirates found themselves without quarry for several weeks. The pirate crew grew angry. Roberts soon discovered the reason for the lack of prey.

In September 1719, a Portuguese fleet of 42 ships had gathered in the Bay of Los Todos Santos, near Salvador, Brazil. The treasure-laden merchantmen planned to sail together as a convoy to Lisbon, Portugal, accompanied by two 70-gun warships. The vessels were filled with untold wealth.

Seeing the Portuguese ships at anchor, Roberts devised a bold plan. He sailed close to one of the smaller ships. The pirate crew took control, threatening the Portuguese captain with death if any distress signal was given. The captain was brought on board the *Rover* and questioned by Roberts. In fear of his life, the captain pointed out which ship carried the greatest booty.

With his target identified, Roberts promptly sailed into action. Keeping the Portuguese captain on board, he sailed straight for the treasure ship. It was a vessel much bigger than the *Rover*, a 40-gun vice-admiral's ship manned by 150 sailors.

To many of the pirates aboard the *Rover*, it must have seemed as though they were sailing towards death. Here was a powerful ship, defended by two nearby men-of-war frigates, and surrounded by many other Portuguese vessels. Was their newly elected captain crazy?

Above: A fleet of ships off the coast of Brazil.

Roberts knew that no one expected this type of brazen attack, least of all the great merchant ship he was approaching. Black Bart placed the kidnapped captain of the smaller ship on deck, forcing him to call out an invitation to the captain of the large treasure-laden vessel. Would he like to come aboard?

The captain became suspicious, but before he could take action, Roberts and his men fired on the ship, threw their grappling hooks, and scrambled aboard. After a brief fight, the pirates took control.

Before the Portuguese warships could come to the rescue, Roberts had sailed away with a fortune in coins, gold chains, jewels, and a cargo of sugar, skins, and tobacco. The plunder even included a gold cross decorated with diamonds—a gift for the king of Portugal. Instead, it would hang from Black Bart's neck as long as the pirate lived.

Code of Conduct

Roberts enjoyed great success that fall day in 1719, but he made a crucial mistake only a few days later. When his ship ran low on food and equipment, Roberts took a small captured sloop and went after a nearby vessel he'd heard was well supplied. There was no need to pay for supplies, Roberts reasoned; he could take what he wanted.

Walter Kennedy, the *Royal Rover*'s quartermaster, and the man who wanted to be captain after Howell Davis was killed, was left in charge of the treasure-filled ship. No sooner had Roberts sailed away, when Kennedy and a group of followers mutinied, taking off in the *Royal Rover*.

Roberts failed to capture the supply ship he'd gone after. When he returned, the *Royal Rover* and his treasure were long gone. It was a hard lesson for the new pirate captain.

Facing Page:
Captain Roberts'
code of conduct.

Roberts probably never knew the fate of Kennedy or the other mutineers. But it would have pleased the captain to know that Kennedy was hated for his treachery, even by those who followed him. The mutineer eventually ended up back home in London. Having spent all his money, Kennedy was arrested for housebreaking. To his great misfortune, the cowardly thief was recognized while in prison, and tried for piracy. His life ended with a noose around his neck on July 19, 1721.

For Captain Roberts, the treachery resulted in his writing the pirates' code of conduct. These 11 articles have become well known over time. Each member of Roberts' crew was expected to sign them and swear an oath of honor to the pirate captain.

Shipboard Articles 1721

Article I. Equal Voting Rights Every man shall have an equal vote in affairs of moment. He shall have an equal title to the fresh provisions or strong liquors at any time seized, and shall use them at pleasure unless a scarcity may make it necessary for the common good that a retrenchment may be voted.

Article II. Fair Shares Every man shall be called fairly in turn by the list on board of prizes, because over and above their proper share, they are allowed a shift of clothes. But if they defraud the company to the value of even one dollar in plate, jewels or money, they shall be marooned. If any man rob another he shall have his nose and ears slit, and be put ashore where he shall be sure to encounter hardships.

Article III. No Gambling None shall game for money either with dice or cards.

Article IV. Lights Out The lights and candles should be put out at eight at night, and if any of the crew desire to drink after that hour they shall sit upon the open deck without lights.

Article V. Weapons Readied Each man shall keep his piece, cutlass and pistols at all times clean and ready for action.

Article VI. No Boys or Women No boy or woman to be allowed amongst them. If any man shall be found seducing any of the latter sex and carrying her to sea in disguise he shall suffer death.

Article VII. Desertion He that shall desert the ship or his quarters in time of battle shall be punished by death or marooning.

Article VIII. Arguments None shall strike another on board the ship, but every man's quarrel shall be ended on shore by sword or pistol in this manner. At the word of command from the quartermaster, each man being previously placed back to back, shall turn and fire immediately. If any man do not, the quartermaster shall knock the piece out of his hand. If both miss their aim they shall take to their cutlasses, and he that draweth first blood shall be declared the victor.

Article IX. Wounded Men No man shall talk of breaking up their way of living till each has a share of 1,000. Every man who shall become a cripple or lose a limb in the service shall have 800 pieces of eight from the common stock and for lesser hurts proportionately.

Article X. Shares of Booty The captain and the quartermaster shall each receive two shares of a prize, the master gunner and boatswain, one and one half shares, all other officers one and one quarter, and private gentlemen of fortune one share each.

Article XI. Musicians The musicians shall have rest on the Sabbath Day only by right. On all other days by favor only.

Tea and Music

Black Bart, with only a small crew aboard his 10-gun sloop the *Fortune*, set sail northward. He soon took four small ships, while at the same time steering clear of a British vessel sent to track him down. The mutineer Kennedy may have stolen his ship and treasure, but Captain Roberts was far from finished.

By 1720, Roberts had acquired a bloodthirsty reputation. Yet, the man was by no means a typical pirate. He drank tea, not rum. He didn't gamble, and didn't want the men on board his ship gambling. He encouraged prayer. He kept musicians on board, who played during battle. He wore elegant fashions, yet carried a cutlass and two pairs of pistols tied at the end of a silk sash. The silk cording was tied to his belt to keep the pistols from dropping overboard during boarding attacks.

Despite all of Roberts' fancy ways, he was neither timid nor merciful. His first pirate flag showed Roberts holding an hourglass with a skeleton clutching a spear. It was clear to Roberts' victims that it was only a matter of time until death, should they choose to defy him.

With only one ship and a crew of 60, Roberts sailed up the eastern coast of North America, heading towards the island of Newfoundland, which today is a province of Canada. In June 1720, Black Bart sailed into Trepassey Bay with his terrifying flag flying, musicians playing, and drums pounding. Frightened fishermen and merchants abandoned their boats and fled inland.

All too easily, Roberts and his pirate crew raided some 26 sloops and 150 fishing boats. Enjoying their reign of terror, the crew also destroyed buildings and machinery along the shoreline. Merchandise and goods not needed or wanted by the pirates were tossed into the ocean.

Ships were burned and sunk, with the exception of one, a 16-gun galley seized by Roberts. With this ship, he later attacked a larger French vessel, which he captured and renamed the *Fortune*. He then captured yet another French ship, a 28-gun warship he renamed the *Royal Fortune*. He would use this name for each successive vessel that became his flagship.

Above: Roberts' ominous flag.

With the powerful *Royal Fortune* under his command, Roberts became bolder in his attacks. Sailing the Atlantic, he and his crew raided at least a dozen English merchant vessels. The pirates became so sure of themselves, and the fear they instilled, they no longer had to plunder and retreat in fear of being caught.

In July 1720, the pirates boarded an English ship called the *Samuel*. Over two days time, the raiders carried off much of the ship's goods, while destroying the rest for no other reason than they wanted to. The *Samuel*'s commander, Captain Cary, was left on board with a few passengers and one other sailor. The rest of his crew was forced to serve aboard the pirate ships.

As Roberts and his crew debated whether to blow up the *Samuel*, another merchant prize was sighted. Roberts quickly sailed off in pursuit. Captain Cary was left to limp into Boston Harbor, where he reported the attack and described the pirate crew as "…more like fiends than men."

Fearless

Throughout the summer of 1720, Roberts and his men plundered ship after ship. Rumors of violence, torture, and murder began to surface. Roberts never stayed very long in one place, being smart enough to keep naval and merchant ships guessing where he might strike next.

In September 1720, Roberts was back in the Caribbean. He sailed into a harbor on the island of St. Kitts, looted one ship, stole a cargo of sheep, and then set fire to two other vessels. The very next day, Roberts re-entered the harbor. This time he was met with cannon fire and was forced to sail off. The following day the pirate captain could not resist sending an insulting letter to the English governor:

> *Had you come off as you ought to a done, and drank a glass of Wine with me and my company, I should not harmed the least vessel in your harbour. Further, it is not your guns you fired that affrighted me or hindered our coming on shore, but the wind….*

Roberts had become fearless. His very presence halted a great deal of shipping in the Caribbean. This was an intolerable problem for the honest people of the West Indies. Governors across the islands sought help from privateers to capture the lawless raiders. However, many pirate hunters feared for their own lives, and refused to hunt Black Bart.

Roberts was furious when he heard that the governors of Barbados and Martinique had offered a reward for his capture. He created a new flag, an image of himself standing in triumph with one foot over a skull that read ABH (A Barbadian's Head) while the other foot stood on a skull that read AMH (A Martinique's Head).

Below: Captain Roberts' flag shows him standing on the skulls of his enemies.

After raiding dozens of French vessels, Roberts boldly took on a French man-of-war. When he boarded the ship, the pirate captain discovered the governor of Martinique among the passengers. With great pleasure, Black Bart hanged him from the yardarm. Some say the pirates even used the governor's body for target practice. To add to the grisly insult, Roberts took over the 52-gun French warship, making it his flagship and renaming it the *Royal Fortune*.

With his captured plunder, Roberts sailed for Africa. Hated and despised from the Caribbean up through North America, Africa was one of the few places where he could still trade his stolen goods for gold. Even there, few wanted to risk trading with him. In fact, the British Piracy Act of 1721 made it illegal to trade with pirates.

These difficulties did not stop Roberts. Many honest sailors and merchants would continue to feel the merciless fury of Black Bart and his piratical crew.

Above: A luckless victim hangs from the yardarm of a ship. The same fate befell the governor of Martinique aboard Roberts' ship.

Fortunes

By 1721, Roberts had amassed a great fortune. French ships were his favorite targets. Dozens of unfortunate victims lost not only their cargo, but also their lives. Many sailors were tortured before they were killed. Some were whipped, or even had their ears cut off.

Black Bart now commanded three ships, the *Fortune*, the *Good Fortune*, and the *Royal Fortune*. But his undisciplined pirate crew members were becoming restless. Roberts had difficulty controlling the murderous raiders.

Thomas Anstis sailed with Roberts as the captain of the *Good Fortune*. He had been with Howell Davis, and stayed with Roberts after Davis' death. However, Anstis was ready to be done with the proud and demanding pirate captain. While sailing for Africa to exchange their captured plunder for gold, Anstis stole away on the *Good Fortune*, taking the crew and booty with him. Roberts, however, had been smart enough to keep the best treasure aboard his own ship. The mutineer Anstis was killed two years later by his own men.

Roberts continued plundering and capturing ship after ship. One prize he kept as a supply ship, renaming it *Little Ranger*. Another was a 32-gun French warship, which he renamed *Great Ranger*.

Roberts' greatest prize was a Royal African Company frigate, the *Onslow*. The ship was loaded with treasure. The happy pirate captain kept the *Onslow* as his flagship, fitting it with 40 guns and once again renaming it *Royal Fortune*.

Roberts had become an even bigger threat to British sea trading. The government was determined to put a stop to the pirate's marauding. By now, both his general location, as well as the ship on which he sailed, were known to the Royal Navy. And they were not afraid of him.

Facing Page: A treasure chest filled with gold, silver, and jewels.

Ransom

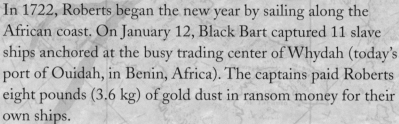

In 1722, Roberts began the new year by sailing along the African coast. On January 12, Black Bart captured 11 slave ships anchored at the busy trading center of Whydah (today's port of Ouidah, in Benin, Africa). The captains paid Roberts eight pounds (3.6 kg) of gold dust in ransom money for their own ships.

One captain foolishly refused to pay. Roberts, in an act of senseless violence, covered the ship's deck in tar and set it ablaze. He felt no need to unload the ship's cargo of 80 slaves. Shackled together in pairs, the unfortunate souls had the choice of burning to death or jumping overboard and being eaten alive by sharks. As the ship burned, Roberts calmly sailed away with the gold ransom, but his day of reckoning was fast approaching.

Several months earlier, two British Royal Navy warships, the HMS *Weymouth* and the HMS *Swallow,* accompanied several merchant ships from England to Africa. The *Swallow* was a formidable two-decker, armed with 50 cannons. After arriving safely with the merchantmen, the two warships began patrolling the African coast.

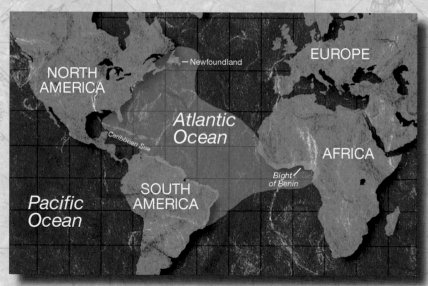

Right: A map of Roberts' piracy range in light blue.

On January 7, 1722, the ships sailed into Cape Coast, a coastal town in Ghana, Africa. Captain Chaloner Ogle, commander of the *Swallow*, learned from the town's governor that pirate ships had been sighted in the area.

Unfortunately, the crew of the *Weymouth* was ravaged with tropical diseases. So many men had come down with malaria, yellow fever, and dysentery that there was not the manpower to sail the ship.

Above: A ship explodes after being attacked by buccaneers.

Captain Ogle set sail with his crew aboard the *Swallow*.

After traveling nearly 200 miles (322 km), Ogle was shocked when he entered the harbor at Whydah on January 15, 1722. It had been just three days since Roberts had sailed off, leaving behind the burned wreckage of his raid. Ogle knew he was close to finding the murderous Black Bart. It was only a matter of time.

Meanwhile, Roberts received warning that warships were cruising the area, looking for him. Roberts wasn't worried. He believed he could stay just out of reach, or if necessary, he would fight the enemy head-on. His ship was well armed, and his men trained for battle.

Into The Sea

Captain Ogle, in command of the Royal Navy ship HMS *Swallow*, learned that the pirate Roberts had stolen a French ship from the port at Whydah. Ogle suspected the raiders would not go far, since they would need to convert their prize into a pirate ship. The nearby Bight (bay) of Benin would be the perfect place. Ogle wrote, "Therefore I judged they must go to some place in Bight to clean and fit the French ship before they would think of cruising again, which occasioned me to steer away into the Bight and look into those places which I knew had depth of water sufficient...."

On February 5, 1722, Ogle spotted three of Roberts' pirate ships anchored just off Cape Lopez, on the west African coast of modern-day Gabon. The *Swallow* approached the pirates, but before he could fire his guns, Ogle had to veer away from a treacherous sandbar called Frenchman's Bank.

Black Bart Roberts saw the *Swallow* approach, then abruptly sail off. He believed it was a merchantman trying to escape the pirates. Roberts sent Captain Skyrm and the 32-gun *Great Ranger* after the mystery vessel.

Aboard the *Swallow*, Captain Ogle realized that the pirates did not know his vessel was actually a well-armed warship. In a brilliant play of strategy, he ordered the *Swallow* to slow down, allowing the pirates to catch up. When the *Great Ranger* sailed close enough, Ogle swung his warship directly in the pirate ship's path and opened fire.

The battle lasted about 90 minutes. The *Great Ranger*'s mast was shattered, and 26 pirates lay dead or wounded. Captain Skyrm had one of his legs shot off.

Above: The battle between Roberts' ship and the Royal Navy ship, HMS *Swallow*.

After taking over the *Great Ranger*, Ogle quickly repaired the damaged vessel and sent it to the Isle of Princes. Meanwhile, Ogle set sail once again for Cape Lopez, hoping to find the elusive Black Bart.

With a select crew of British sailors, Ogle arrived back at Cape Lopez a few days later. Roberts' ships were right where Ogle had last seen them. In fact, Bartholomew Roberts was in the midst of a great on-board celebration. His crew was drinking heavily, and he was busy entertaining several merchants.

Ogle waited patiently until dawn on February 10, 1722. In the driving rain, the British warship approached the pirates. Ogle hoisted a French flag, which confused the pirates aboard the *Royal Fortune*. Was this new arrival a slave ship? Or Captain Skyrm returning in a captured vessel? One pirate, a deserter from the *Swallow*, recognized his old ship and tried to warn anyone who would listen. But nothing was done until it was too late. On Captain Ogle's orders, the *Swallow*'s guns were readied, the French flag lowered, and the British flag run up the mast. At that point, the pirates knew they were in deep trouble.

To prepare for battle, Roberts dressed in his finery, donning his pistols and cutlass. As thunder and lightning crashed from the sky, Black Bart ordered the *Royal Fortune* to sail directly at the enemy ship.

Above: Black Bart Roberts is killed by grapeshot. Following their captain's standing order, the pirates threw his body into the sea.

The captain and crew of the powerful *Swallow* were prepared for a fight. Through the driving rain, each ship fired at the other.

As the smoke cleared, the pirates discovered that their beloved captain's luck had finally run out. Bartholomew Roberts' body was slumped over a cannon, his throat torn out by grapeshot from the *Swallow*'s cannon.

Bartholomew Roberts had a standing order that if he died in battle, his crew should throw his body overboard. Roberts feared that his corpse would be displayed in public as a warning to pirates, which was the custom at the time. The buccaneers quickly carried out Roberts' last request. Dressed in all his finery, the pirate's bloody corpse sank into the murky sea, down to the depths of Davy Jones' locker. Shortly afterwards, the pirate crew surrendered.

Captain Ogle didn't lose a single man in the fight with Roberts. Back home in England, he became a national hero and received a knighthood. Of the pirate crew, 52 were hanged, 70 black pirates were sent into slavery, 37 received lesser sentences and 74 were freed, having proven they were forced into piracy.

Thus ended Roberts' reign of terror on the high seas. He was finally dead, a fitting end for the pirate captain who once said, "No, a merry life and a short one shall be my motto."

In less than 32 months, Bartholomew Roberts terrorized ships all over the Atlantic Ocean, raiding 400 vessels and killing hundreds of people. He was a master mariner, a man of learning and culture. But Roberts was also a thief and a bloodthirsty killer, one of the most fearsome buccaneers in the Golden Age of Piracy.

Glossary

Booty
Money, jewels, and other valuables seized off a ship by raiding pirates.

Caribbean
The islands and area of the Caribbean Sea, roughly the area between Florida and South and Central America.

Cutlass
A short, curved sword having a single sharp edge, often used by seamen.

Davy Jones' Locker
A centuries-old phrase of unknown origin meaning "the bottom of the ocean."

Dysentery
An infectious disease characterized by severe diarrhea.

Flagship
The largest and most important ship in a fleet. Also, the ship that the commander of a fleet sails on.

Frigate
A sailing warship, smaller and faster than a man-of-war, usually used to protect merchant ships or other warships.

Golden Age of Piracy
Roughly the years 1660 to 1740, the era when piracy was at its peak, especially along the coast of colonial America and in the Caribbean. Many former privateers, put out of work as peace spread across Europe, turned to piracy as a lucrative lifestyle. The lack of a strong, central colonial government led to poor protection of ships at sea, at a time when many vessels carried valuables across the Atlantic.

Grapeshot
A weapon consisting of a cluster of small iron balls loaded into a canvas bag. The collection of balls resembled a cluster of grapes. Shot from a cannon, the balls spread out from the muzzle at high velocity, killing or injuring anyone hit.

Letter of Marque

Official government document granting a ship captain permission to use his personal armed vessel for capturing and raiding ships of another country. Used by governments to expand their naval forces at a time of war.

Malaria

A serious, sometimes fatal disease found in tropical regions. In the 18th century malaria was quite deadly, and thought to be caused from breathing the foul air around swamps and stagnant water. In fact, people get malaria when an infected mosquito bites them. Malaria infections cause flu-like symptoms such as high fever, chills, muscle pain, and diarrhea.

Man-of-War

A large sailing warship armed with many cannons. Men-of-war were used on the front line of a battle.

Pirates

Rugged outlaw seamen who capture and raid ships at sea to seize their cargo and other valuables.

Privateer

A ship, or its captain and crew, operating under a letter of marque. A country issues letters of marque to permit the raiding of ships from specified countries that it has engaged in war. The captain and crew were paid out of any booty they took from the ships they attacked.

Yardarm

On a sailing ship, a long, horizontal pole made of wood and tapered toward the ends, used to support and spread a square sail.

Yellow Fever

A disease that causes damage to the liver, kidney, heart and intestines. The name comes from one of its symptoms, jaundice, or yellowing of the skin. Yellow fever occurs most often in tropical climates, and is spread through bites of infected mosquitos. A disease that once caused thousands of deaths, yellow fever is now limited to unvaccinated populations in some developing nations.

Index

Up the Anchor by Don Maitz.